LAURA K. MURRAY

BIGFOOT

ARE THEY REAL?

CREATIVE EDUCATION · CREATIVE PAPERBACKS

Published by Creative Education and Creative Paperbacks

P.O. Box 227, Mankato, Minnesota 56002

Creative Education and Creative Paperbacks are imprints of The Creative Company

www.thecreativecompany.us

Design and production by **Christine Vanderbeek**

Art direction by **Rita Marshall**

Printed in the United States of America

Photographs by Alamy (AMBLIN/UNIVERSAL/Ronald Grant Archive, Bill Brooks, William Manning, Dale O'Dell, UDA, United Archives GmbH), Corbis (Antonino Barbagallo, Bettmann), Dreamstime (James Steidl), iStockphoto (Sam Camp, Rich Legg, Roberto A Sanchez, wwing), Shutterstock (AlexussK, GUDKOV ANDREY, BestGreenScreen, Dragan85, Sergey Mironov, Ken Nyborg, PHOTO BY LOLA, Olha Rohulya, seregalsv, tele52, Josemaria Toscano)

Library of Congress Cataloging-in-Publication Data

Murray, Laura K.   Bigfoot / Laura K. Murray.   p. cm. – (Are they real?)   Includes index.   Summary: A high-interest inquiry into the possible existence of North America's forest-dwelling Bigfoot, emphasizing reported sightings and seekers as well as footprint analyses.

ISBN 978-1-60818-761-4 (hardcover)   **ISBN 978-1-62832-369-6** (pbk)   **ISBN 978-1-56660-803-9** (ebook)

1. Sasquatch–Juvenile literature.

QL89.2.S2 M877 2017

001.944–dc23   2016008267

CCSS: RI.1.1, 2, 4, 5, 6, 7, 10; RI.2.1, 2, 4, 5, 6, 7; RI.3.1, 2, 5, 6, 7; RF.1.1, 2, 3, 4; RF.2.3, 4; RF.3.3, 4

First Edition HC 9 8 7 6 5 4 3 2 1   **First Edition PBK** 9 8 7 6 5 4 3 2 1

CONTENTS

A SIGHTING. 4

SHY SASQUATCH 6

WHAT DOES BIGFOOT LOOK LIKE? 8

WHAT DOES BIGFOOT DO? 10

STORIES OF BIGFOOT. 14

BIGFOOT ENCOUNTERS 18

INVESTIGATE IT! TRACKING BIGFOOT 22

GLOSSARY. 24   WEBSITES 24

READ MORE 24   INDEX. 24

A SIGHTING

Roger Patterson and Bob Gimlin are riding horses in California. They see a tall, hairy figure near a creek. The men chase after it!

THE BEAST DISAPPEARS INTO THE WOODS.

SHY SASQUATCH

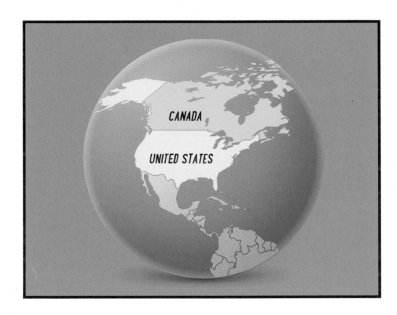

Some people think Bigfoot is a huge, shy creature that walks on two feet. Bigfoot is said to live in the United States and Canada. It hides deep in forests. Some people call it "Sasquatch."

6

WHAT DOES BIGFOOT LOOK LIKE?

Bigfoot is named for its big feet. But its body is probably big, too.

It is 6.5 to 10 feet (2–3 m) tall! Bigfoot might look like an **APE** with dark hair.

Its eyes shine at night. It smells terrible.

9

WHAT DOES BIGFOOT DO?

Many people think they have seen Bigfoot. Maybe they really saw a bear.

IS THAT BIGFOOT OR A BEAR?

Some people have found strange footprints, hair, and droppings in the woods. What left them there?

Grover Krantz was a **SCIENTIST**. He was one of the first people to study Bigfoot. He looked closely at footprints. He said Bigfoot was a kind of ape.

GROVER KRANTZ

12

GORILLAS ARE APES.

STORIES OF BIGFOOT

In 1958, a man named Jerry Crew found giant footprints in California.

People named the unknown creature "Bigfoot." Was it a **HOAX**?

There are TV shows about the real-life hunt for Bigfoot. Bigfoot stars in movies like *Harry and the Hendersons*, too.

Places around the world have stories about animals like Bigfoot!

BIGFOOT ENCOUNTERS

People try to find **PROOF** of Bigfoot. They set up cameras that see in the dark. They use **DRONES** to search the forests. But maybe Bigfoot wants to stay hidden.

What would you do
if you saw Bigfoot?

PLUG YOUR NOSE AND BACK AWAY!

INVESTIGATE IT!
TRACKING BIGFOOT

Have you ever seen animal tracks? You might find them at the park or in your own yard. Learn more at www.biokids.umich.edu/guides/tracks_and _sign/. Then get outside to explore! What do you think Bigfoot's tracks would look like?

WHAT DO YOU THINK MADE THIS TRACK? THE ANSWER IS BELOW.

GLOSSARY

APE a large animal like a gorilla or chimpanzee

DRONES aircraft flown by people on the ground

HOAX a joke or prank

PROOF information that shows something is true

SCIENTIST a person who studies how the world works

READ MORE

Perish, Patrick. *Is Bigfoot Real?* Mankato, Minn.: Amicus, 2014.

Theisen, Paul. *Bigfoot.* Minneapolis: Bellwether Media, 2011.

WEBSITES

Animal Tracks: Is Bigfoot Real?
http://campfire.andycamper.com/the-weird-outdoors-is-bigfoot-real
Watch a video on Bigfoot, and learn more about tracking.

Finding Bigfoot
http://discoverykids.com/games/finding-bigfoot/
Play a game and pretend to be Bigfoot.

Note: Every effort has been made to ensure that the websites listed above are suitable for children, that they have educational value, and that they contain no inappropriate material. However, because of the nature of the Internet, it is impossible to guarantee that these sites will remain active indefinitely or that their contents will not be altered.

INDEX

apes 9, 12

cameras and drones 18

Canada 6

Crew, Jerry 14

eyes 9

footprints 11, 12, 14, 22

forests 6, 18

Gimlin, Bob 4

hair 4, 9, 11

Harry and the Hendersons 16

Krantz, Grover 12

Patterson, Roger 4

size 8, 9

smell 9, 21

United States 4, 6, 14